Life Cycle

Frogs

Aaron Carr

LET'S READ

AV² BY WEIGL™

ADDED VALUE · AUDIO VISUAL

www.av2books.com

LET'S READ AV²
BY WEIGL™
ADDED VALUE • AUDIO VISUAL

Go to **www.av2books.com**, and enter this book's unique code.

BOOK CODE

U555650

AV² by Weigl brings you media enhanced books that support active learning.

AV² provides enriched content that supplements and complements this book. Weigl's AV² books strive to create inspired learning and engage young minds in a total learning experience.

Your AV² Media Enhanced books come alive with...

Audio
Listen to sections of the book read aloud.

Video
Watch informative video clips.

Embedded Weblinks
Gain additional information for research.

Try This!
Complete activities and hands-on experiments.

Key Words
Study vocabulary, and complete a matching word activity.

Quizzes
Test your knowledge.

Slide Show
View images and captions, and prepare a presentation.

... and much, much more!

Published by AV² by Weigl
350 5th Avenue, 59th Floor New York, NY 10118
Website: www.av2books.com   www.weigl.com

Library of Congress Control Number: 2013934645
ISBN 978-1-62127-685-2 (hardcover)
ISBN 978-1-62127-686-9 (softcover)

Printed in the United States of America in North Mankato, Minnesota
1 2 3 4 5 6 7 8 9 0 17 16 15 14 13

032013
WEP300113

Senior Editor: Aaron Carr
Art Director: Terry Paulhus

Weigl acknowledges Getty Images as the primary image supplier for this title.

SCIENCE KIDS
Life Cycles

Frogs

CONTENTS

All animals begin life, grow, and make more animals. This is a life cycle.

Frogs are amphibians. Amphibians are cold-blooded animals. This means they need the Sun to keep them warm.

Frogs are born in water. They hatch from eggs when they are born.

Red-eyed tree frog eggs hang from plants. The baby frogs fall into the water when the eggs hatch.

Baby frogs are called tadpoles. They look like small fish. Tadpoles breathe under water.

11

It takes tadpoles about eight weeks to grow into froglets. Froglets grow legs and begin to lose their tails.

A froglet looks like a small frog with a tail.

Froglets can leave the water after about 12 weeks. They grow lungs to let them breathe air. Many frogs breathe through their skin.

Frogs are fully grown by about 16 weeks old. They are now ready to make more frogs.

Frogs lay their eggs in large clumps called spawns. A frog spawn has many eggs covered in clear jelly. Some frogs can lay up to 20,000 eggs at one time.

There are about 5,400 kinds of frogs. Each kind of frog may be a different color or size. The color and size of a frog comes from its parents.

Life Cycles Quiz

Test your knowledge of frog life cycles by taking this quiz. Look at these pictures. Which stage of the life cycle do you see in each picture?

KEY WORDS

Research has shown that as much as 65 percent of all written material published in English is made up of 300 words. These 300 words cannot be taught using pictures or learned by sounding them out. They must be recognized by sight. This book contains 59 common sight words to help young readers improve their reading fluency and comprehension. This book also teaches young readers several important content words, such as proper nouns. These words are paired with pictures to aid in learning and improve understanding.

Page	Sight Words First Appearance	Page	Content Words First Appearance
5	a, all, and, animals, grow, is, life, make, more, this	5	life cycle
6	are, keep, means, need, the, them, they, to	6	amphibians, frogs, Sun
9	from, in, into, plants, water, when	9	baby, eggs, red-eyed tree frog
11	like, look, small, under	11	fish, tadpoles
13	about, takes, their, with	13	froglets, legs, tails, weeks
14	after, air, can, leave, let, many, through	14	lungs, skin
16	by, now, old	19	clumps, jelly, spawns
19	at, has, large, one, some, time, up	20	color, parents, size
20	be, comes, different, each, its, kinds, may, of, or, there		

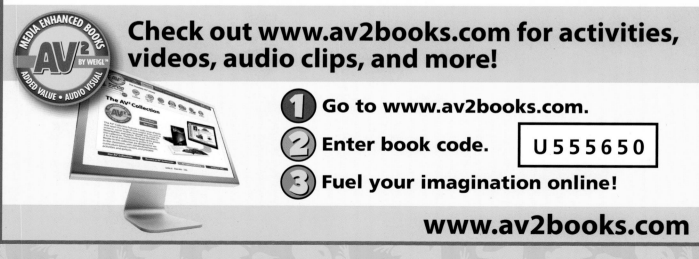

Check out www.av2books.com for activities, videos, audio clips, and more!

1 Go to www.av2books.com.

2 Enter book code. U 5 5 5 6 5 0

3 Fuel your imagination online!

www.av2books.com